Houdini Was...

by

Second Grade Students at
white Bluffs Elementary

(A True Story!)

Scholastic Inc.
New York   Toronto   London   Auckland   Sydney   Mexico City   New Delhi   Hong Kong   Buenos Aires

Dedicated to. . .

all classroom pets great and small
who teach us responsibility, compassion
and unconditional love.

Houdini was. . .

our class pet in room 221 at
White Bluffs Elementary,

She was. . .

except on her ears,
which were speckled hairless saucers.

The only thing small
about her. . .

was her stubby little tail that was

as bald as a plain hot dog.

She escaped too many times
to count,

and when not on the run. . .

with anything valuable, especially. . . carrots

Houdini died today,

but here's the deal. .

we are choosing to be
"HAPPY"

and this is why. . .

Houdini was MORE than just a classroom pet.

She was our SUPERHERO!

he could scale the sides of her cage, leap off a three drawer
file cabinet and zip down 24 steps in the blink of an eye!

She was an
ESCAPE ARTIST. . .

a master at forcing the lid off her ball and
unlocking any hinge made by mankind.

She was a SPY. . .

sneaky night crawler that had a secret spy room
in every corner cabinet in each classroom.

She was an ATHLETE. . .

shooting down the halls as fast as a bullet and able
do pull ups with one paw from the top of her cage

She was a silly CLOWN. . .

climbing the rails of her cage like a monkey
in the circus, while wearing a funny costume

She was an
EXPERT EATER. . .

eagerly munching carrots, lettuce, peas, corn, AND/OR sunflower seeds EVERY WAKING MOMENT!

But most importantly,

she was a member of our classroom FAMILY.

Her innocent looks, sweet little squeaks and twitchy long whiskers warmed our hearts each and every day.

As you can see, that little creature was more than a classroom pet. . .

she was family.

Houdini taught us to. . .
never give up,

to eat our vegetables,

nd to love unconditionally.

As a wise person
once said. . .

"Don't cry that it's over. . .

be happy that it happened."

Thank you, Houdini. . . for happening.

(Houdini hid a carrot in each picture. Can you find her favorite treat? Good luck!)

Kids Are Authors®
Books written by children for children

The Kids Are Authors® Competition was established in 1986 to encourage children to read and to become involved
in the creative process of writing.

Since then, thousands of children have written and illustrated books as participants in the Kids Are Authors® Competition.

The winning books in the annual competition are published by Scholastic Inc.
and are distributed by Scholastic Book Fairs throughout the United States.

For more information:

Kids Are Authors® 1080 Greenwood Blvd.; Lake Mary, FL 32746 or visit our web site at: www.scholastic.com/kidsareauthors

ISBN 13: 978-0-545-29814-8   12 11 10 9 8 7 6 5 4 3 2 1

Cover design by Bill Henderson

Printed and bound in the U.S.A.   First Printing, July 2010